AF479030

It's a musical wonderland…
tiptoeing through clouds
go color of intrigue into minds
yes indeed this is something
that all people of the world need…

Welcome to

Lost
Journey

Library of Congress Cataloging in Publication Data

Robinson, D. Jimmy

Lost Journey—1st ed.
Jimmyland Corporation

ISBN: 0-9760140-2-5

Printed in the United States of America

CONTENTS

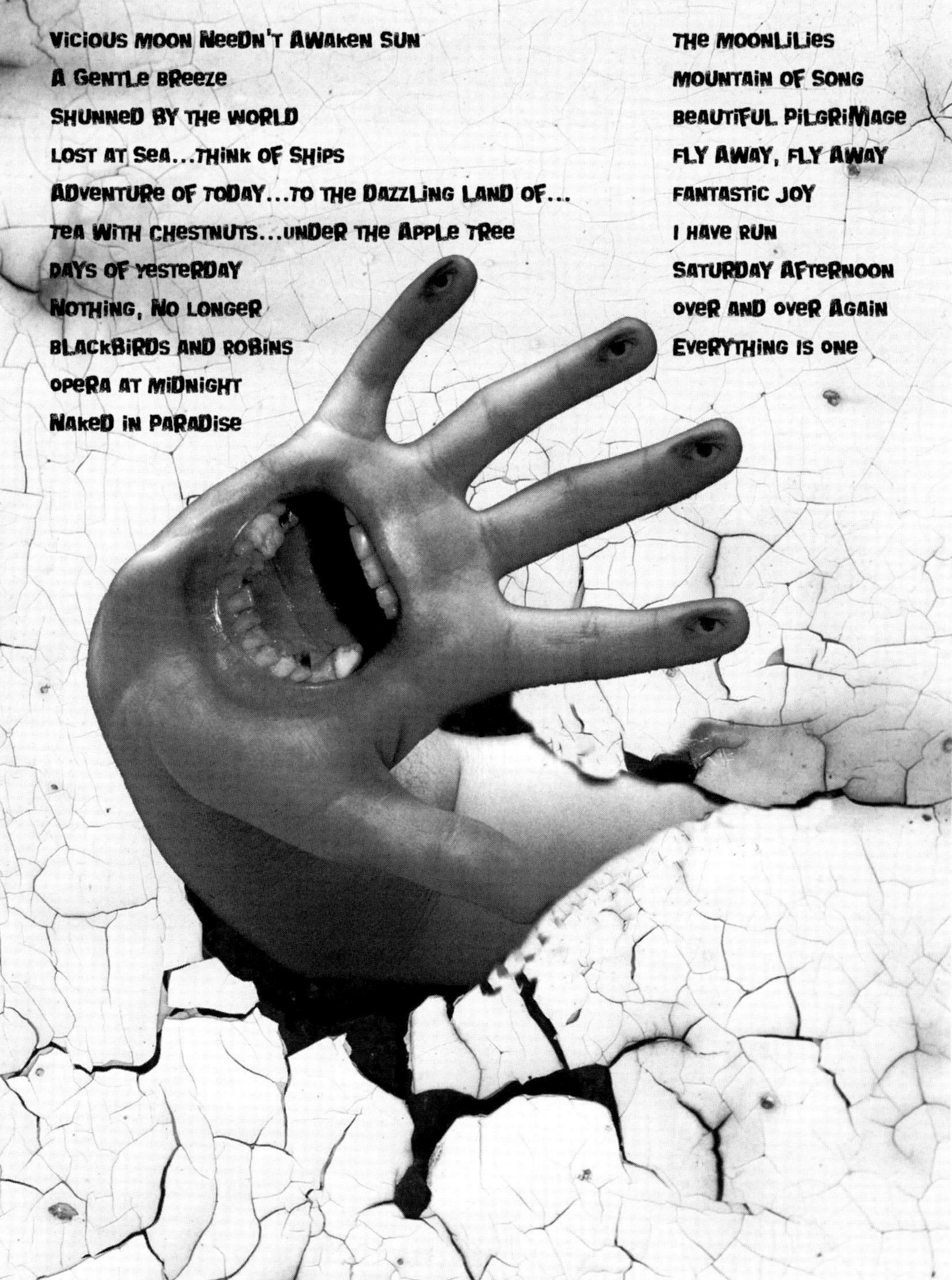

VICIOUS MOON NEEDN'T AWAKEN SUN

Dark and weary I sit.
Blood drips from the haunted desire,
And into lonesome teardrops.
Splendid spectacle of riddles
Ominous presence of late night soiree.
Vicious moon needn't awaken sun.
Cobblestone streets eerie sensation,
Provokes venom to topple and swath
Glistening smiles of crisp music.
A peek-a-boo from remotest corner
Cracks the chimney.
For Christ's sake everything isn't studded with stars.
Labyrinth in time . . . Black roses afar
Sudden rendezvous . . . Crisp mandarin trickling.

Foreboding specter from the past
Grim drama unfolds . . .
Violin playing in the night.

Deeper into the Castle of Mystery
S C R E A M S . . .
A morning with . . .

Soft glow in the crackling fire
Escapes hands of yesterday.

A Gentle Breeze

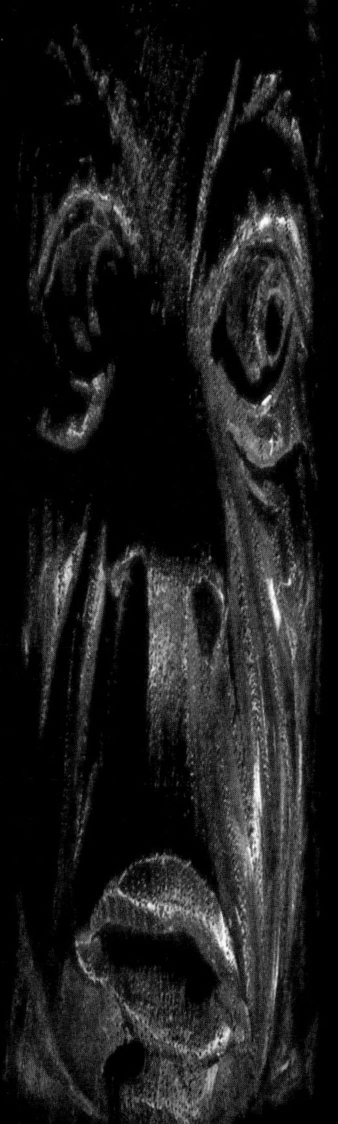

Good natured sarcasm soaring
Through the poetry...Sudden recollection
Of a brilliant moon alone with
Footsteps of peace.
Glistening crispness of morning dew.
Eerie sensation surged into the blood
Of a wicked grin....
Sprinkling of winter rendezvous.
Sudden burning of desire melts
Witches into the throne.

Cast a shadow...Cripple the storm...
Mind a century old.
Saharan camels
Deadly are their cries...

Fingertips reaching for a song of rhyme.

A gentle breeze...The desert storm.
Away goes their souls
To gather....

Roses of a thorn

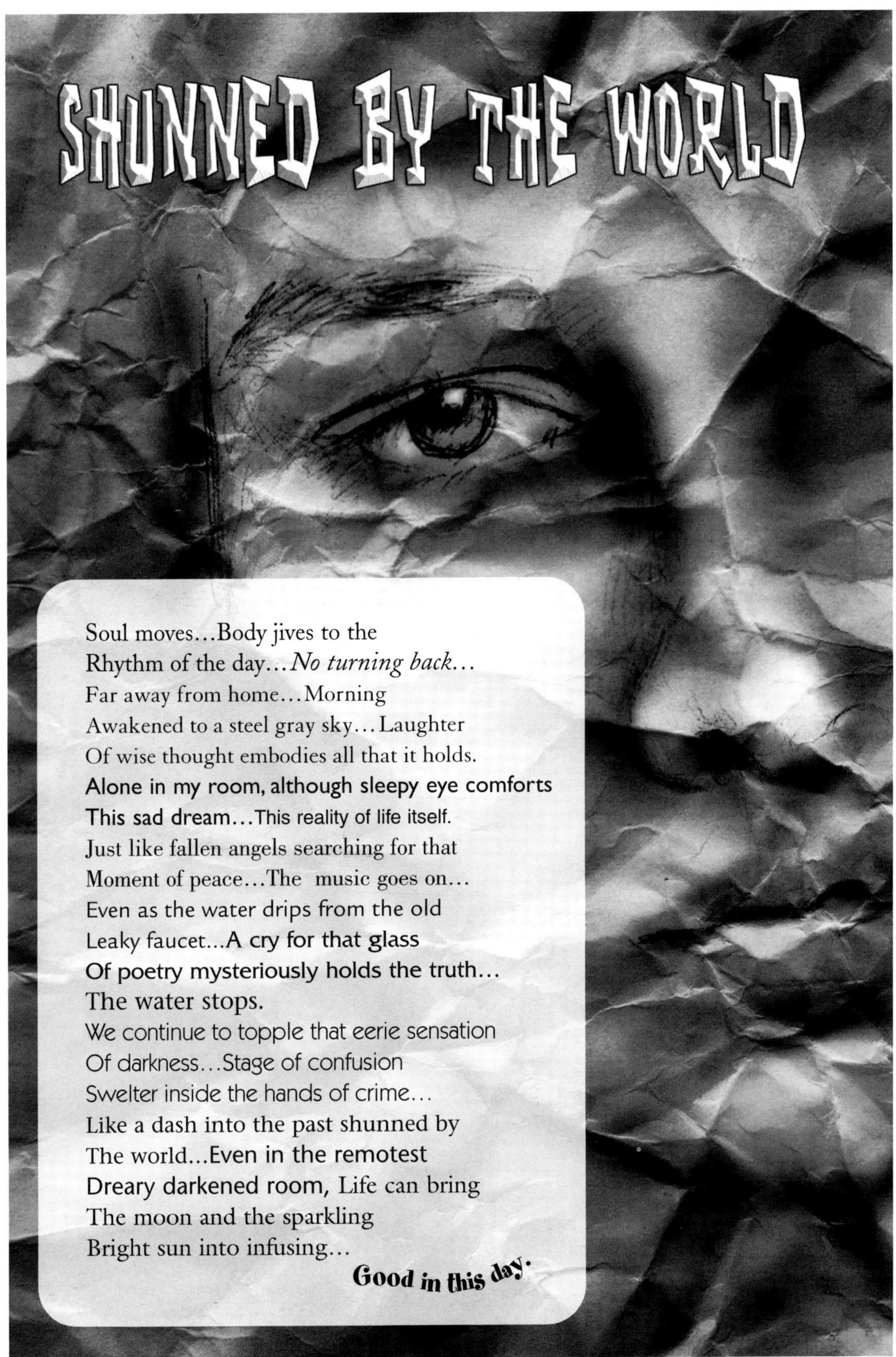

SHUNNED BY THE WORLD

Soul moves…Body jives to the
Rhythm of the day…*No turning back…*
Far away from home…Morning
Awakened to a steel gray sky…Laughter
Of wise thought embodies all that it holds.
Alone in my room, although sleepy eye comforts
This sad dream…This reality of life itself.
Just like fallen angels searching for that
Moment of peace…The music goes on…
Even as the water drips from the old
Leaky faucet…A cry for that glass
Of poetry mysteriously holds the truth…
The water stops.
We continue to topple that eerie sensation
Of darkness…Stage of confusion
Swelter inside the hands of crime…
Like a dash into the past shunned by
The world…Even in the remotest
Dreary darkened room, Life can bring
The moon and the sparkling
Bright sun into infusing…

Good in this day.

LOST AT SEA...
Think of Ships

Innocence.
A chestnut of desire.
Quivering against untamed cruelty
Ships the moon.
Silent are the whispers.

Gentle is the breeze.
Phoenix soaring toward the sun...
Sudden curiosity evokes madness.
Chuckles of gingerly cute smiles
Collided the oceans, which glimmer past
Bursting with joy, but stunned by the dragons tear swept cry
The Queen, dancing with a mocking bird
Elegance whispers
Good Morning

Battle behind mysterious fate of joy.
Wrinkled feathers
Just a painted picture behind the sun
Encircling the moon.
Mystery the feet of time.
Stunned vanished into gloom...webs of leaves
Sprinkle...black velvet whispers

Battle in the night...
Revenge of eighty nights...
   of unhappily
Lost in the grayness of the sea...
Think of ships
Think of waves of peace.
Anchored
A junkyard of stone
Bloodened by the ominous thought
Dreams falter by wayside of ships, and callous hands
Creeping further onto the grayest bridge
Tumbling down forever...
Graves of music
Awaken the roses

ADVENTURE OF TODAY.

To the Dazzling Land of...

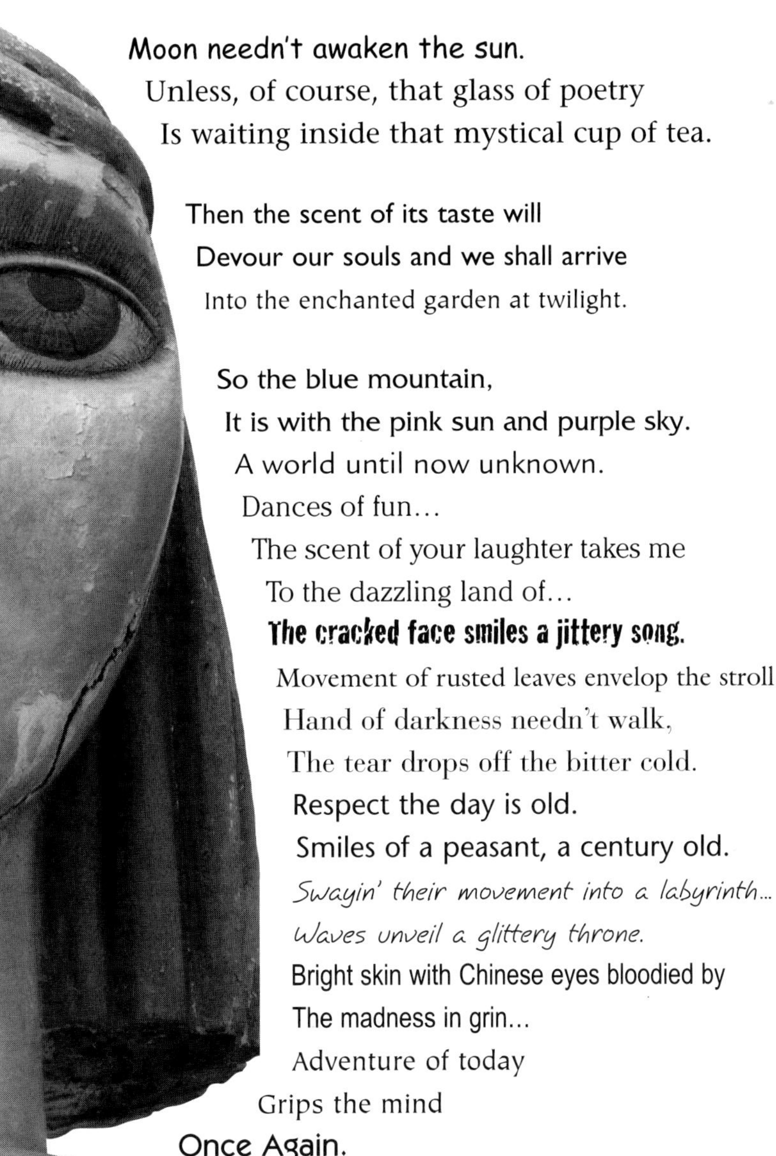

Moon needn't awaken the sun.
Unless, of course, that glass of poetry
Is waiting inside that mystical cup of tea.

Then the scent of its taste will
Devour our souls and we shall arrive
Into the enchanted garden at twilight.

So the blue mountain,
It is with the pink sun and purple sky.
A world until now unknown.
Dances of fun…
The scent of your laughter takes me
To the dazzling land of…
The cracked face smiles a jittery song.
Movement of rusted leaves envelop the stroll.
Hand of darkness needn't walk,
The tear drops off the bitter cold.
Respect the day is old.
Smiles of a peasant, a century old.
Swayin' their movement into a labyrinth…
Waves unveil a glittery throne.
Bright skin with Chinese eyes bloodied by
The madness in grin...
Adventure of today
Grips the mind
Once Again.

Tea with Chestnuts... Under the Apple Tree

Tea with chestnuts under the apple tree.
Dashing azure sky billowing above and
Soft music lost in our eyes. Our brown and
Blue jewels which transfix the color of the
Earth into a beautiful place for us
To see every day.
Hands like four leaf clovers reaching
Up and picking the apples.
Their golden shape round and yet
Deliciously wide.
Juices bittersweet exploding and
Brushing the breeze with candy apple smiles.
Yummy and yawns after the tummy
Enjoys the scouring flavor of the fruit.
To sleep…
Song awakened strings of time…
Riddled in the glistening sun,
Stillness, an owl peeks over
The crooked branch. *Laughter of*
Nature's presence.
Crickets, whiskers, and white buttons.
Simple harmony…
Flower colors the green grass.
Forest…a walk under the apple tree.

DAYS OF YESTERDAY

Vanished forever the vein of misery
Reaps of a hallow mind.
Splendid spectacle of days of
Yesterday caught in an ominous
Dance with a black spider.
Ungracious sardonic wine.
The symphony that topples
Crisp breeze of morning.

Dangled the diamonds off
The garden's tree with their
Beauty riddled in crime.
Blistering confines with dark cubes…
Ostracized by the sun and the moon
Bloodened the tear drops of joy
Took the clock's wings
Waves of lies embedded in time.
No strawberries to eat.
Music lost its beat
Age lines ungraced the throne.

NOTHING, NO LONGER

Desolate is the laughter. Voices lost in time.
Walls of darkness echo nothing.
Seemingly unforgettable song, creepy
And eerie no longer.
A bell chimes.
Swept away traveling into the night
Rapture evokes glare.
Repertoire of moon.
Vision of unreasoning sorrow.
Daffodils bloom in the wildest grave.

Ballerinas, dragons, bees and swans.
Shining battle in the mind
Mysteriously fluttering waves
Softly into sublime.

Manipulate rising after peeks of time
Gingerly kisses colliding with
Cluster of fear.

Nothing, no longer.

Separates sky from morning
Cries from moonlight
Angels from death
Nothing, no longer.

Nothing, no longer.

No more clusters of tears

BLACKBIRDS AND ROBINS

SHINING FOOTSTEPS IN CREATURES WHICH LURK ABOUT
Paint visions of darkness into waves of sound...
Blackbirds and robins and crystal clear morning dew

Fascinated by the masquerade...daunting these footsteps

CHARCOAL BLACK IS THE NIGHT,

Writing songs shake the misery of time

DREAMY, DREARY AND BLUE

Moon casting shadows
Knights white tiger-eyes aglow... curse from beyond
wings of kisses grow wildly so

GHOULS' WIDE WHISPERS IN DUSTY CLOSETS SWEEPING
THE BLOODENED POETRY OUT OF THE SOUL

Knights in steel capers
A long way from home

Crown the castle
Sea of memory swept away
Shake the misery of time
Moon needn't awaken the sun

FLY AWAY BLACKBIRDS AND ROBINS FLY AWAY

Opera at Midnight

Ripening beneath splendid
Rich smiles. Ivory pearl
Fingertips ribbon the breeze…
Romantic contrasts open Cupid's glance.
Drawn by desire: A window to the world…
Shepherds unspoken song.
Whip the bitter cold.
Blood and tears tossed with sorrow inspire
The darkness to melt away.
Radiance of the sparkling sun
Rejuvenates sleepy eye…
Sugar coat the opera to enhance
The flavor of the day…
Messenger of the wild. Tangled like a
String. Wine from that ancient plea.

Blackberries and multi colored times
Erupt on the stage.
At midnight perfectly fine.
Reappear relight forest green
Flower joy fantastic
Beneath the moon
Cheers heavenly desired.
Music is made at last.

NAKED IN PARADISE

The zill flower is dripping from my toes.
The green grass is awesome. Just like
A chilled glass of water.
The moonlight is in the reaches of
My hands.
Thought melancholic...sublime
Rose petals...soft winter breeze
Endlessly romantic. Can't remember a
Day without you near.
Lifting the burden...Sifting the ashes
Gates closed the harmony
Needn't ask anymore.
Love without leaving to touch without
Feeling...have to start over again.
Started feeling...wanted you near again.

Barrels of diamonds lay claim
To the apple orchard
Recount footsteps: never be ashamed.
Just trails of fame.
Honesty pieces together
The cracked face.

Heaven knows if you change
Your life
Butterflies will.
Naked in paradise once again.

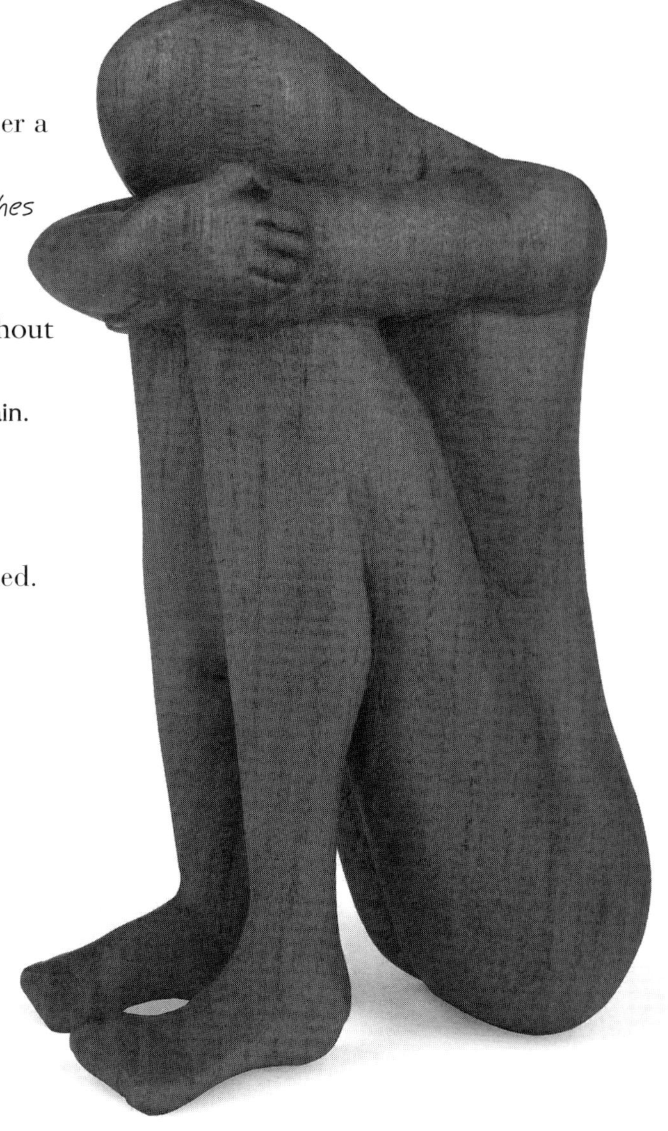

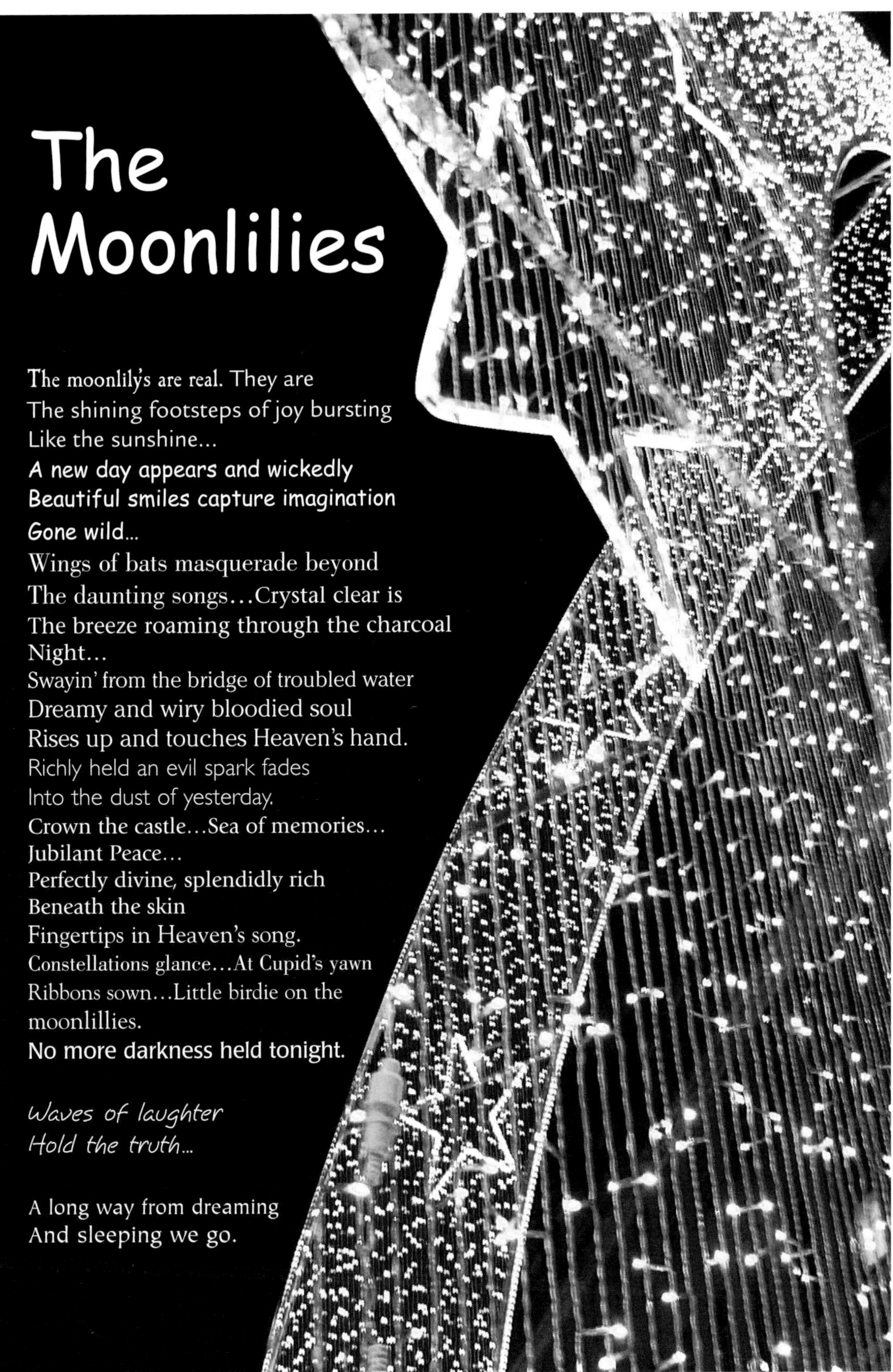

The Moonlilies

The moonlily's are real. They are
The shining footsteps of joy bursting
Like the sunshine...
A new day appears and wickedly
Beautiful smiles capture imagination
Gone wild...
Wings of bats masquerade beyond
The daunting songs...Crystal clear is
The breeze roaming through the charcoal
Night...
Swayin' from the bridge of troubled water
Dreamy and wiry bloodied soul
Rises up and touches Heaven's hand.
Richly held an evil spark fades
Into the dust of yesterday.
Crown the castle...Sea of memories...
Jubilant Peace...
Perfectly divine, splendidly rich
Beneath the skin
Fingertips in Heaven's song.
Constellations glance...At Cupid's yawn
Ribbons sown...Little birdie on the
moonlillies.
No more darkness held tonight.

Waves of laughter
Hold the truth...

A long way from dreaming
And sleeping we go.

Mountain of Song

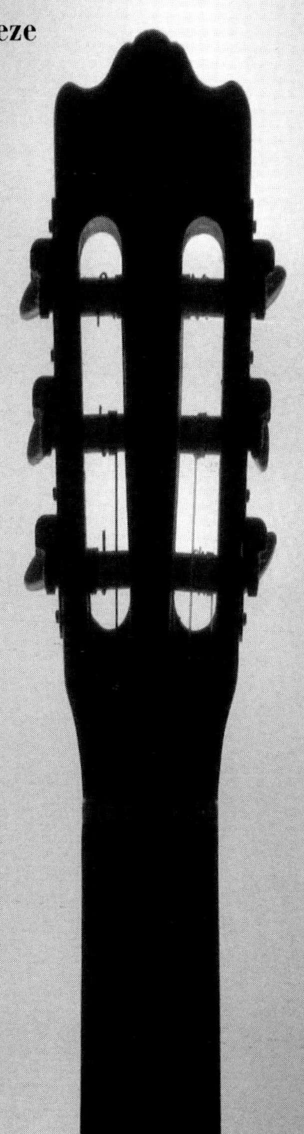

Shadows bursting, flames into the gentle breeze
Clash a dream—fade away—Collapse
Yesterday's memories...Tidal wave ships
The moon...Creepy eyes wave dance
Into the noon day fun...Priggish
Wickedness swallow oligophagus
Cricket.
Bestow enrapture glow...Marmalade time
Eclipse into sublime...Tangle vanish,
Grips of crime...
Swing loose—Disentangle
Vigorous winsome spinet of darkness.

Ripened is the sun. As my heart
Follows sleepy eye into infusing
Good in this day...

Enchanted Garden—Days of yesterday
Moon swept fear...Tea with chestnuts
Adventure of today...Guide the ship
Blackbirds and Robins.

All just widen thought...

Swept into the mountain
Of song writing ways.

Beautiful Pilgrimage

A string dangles in the hands of time.
Pushing the deviance like a serpent into
Rafters of sublime. What's in front
A mountain of disguise. Eyes back
From far beyond. Trying desperately to
Awaken tomorrow's song.
Watching from a window, creped with blood
Hands dangle soft-spoken memories.
Wide moon is bright. Creepy ghoul
Daunts rafters of cries. Beautiful
Pilgrimage. Instrument of strings.
Zither.
Music dances into the fingertips of life
Webs billowing dust from angel's breath
Sprinkle morning awakened sleepy eye
No more tears. No more soft spoken lies.
Turn back—Go Away!
Oceans of black.
Shed the blanket rise above tumultuous
Steel gray sky…branches wither
A hymn…bittersweet never-ending
Shines.

Deep into a forest of sunlight.

Fly Away, Fly Away

Creeping through the webs of darkness
Sweet memories of yesterday
Lurk about…Not a peep from an
angel…
Not a composed sound.
Moon drags thought out of daunted fears
…Without swoon…
Billowing fingers a century old,
Brooms sweep out of closets to bite your head.

Walk through the garden…Dust of days
Gone by…Turn skeletons
Hands bloodied red…

  …Drip…
    …Drip…
      …Drip…

A basket of time
Mixed with the porridge
Black cats whiskers wide.
Hills and valleys
Steep below…
Beyond the cries…

Bitter tides seemingly
Unforgettable song…
Withered away…
Midnight fallen asleep.

<u>Guide The Ship</u>
  …Drip…
    …Drip…
      …Drip…

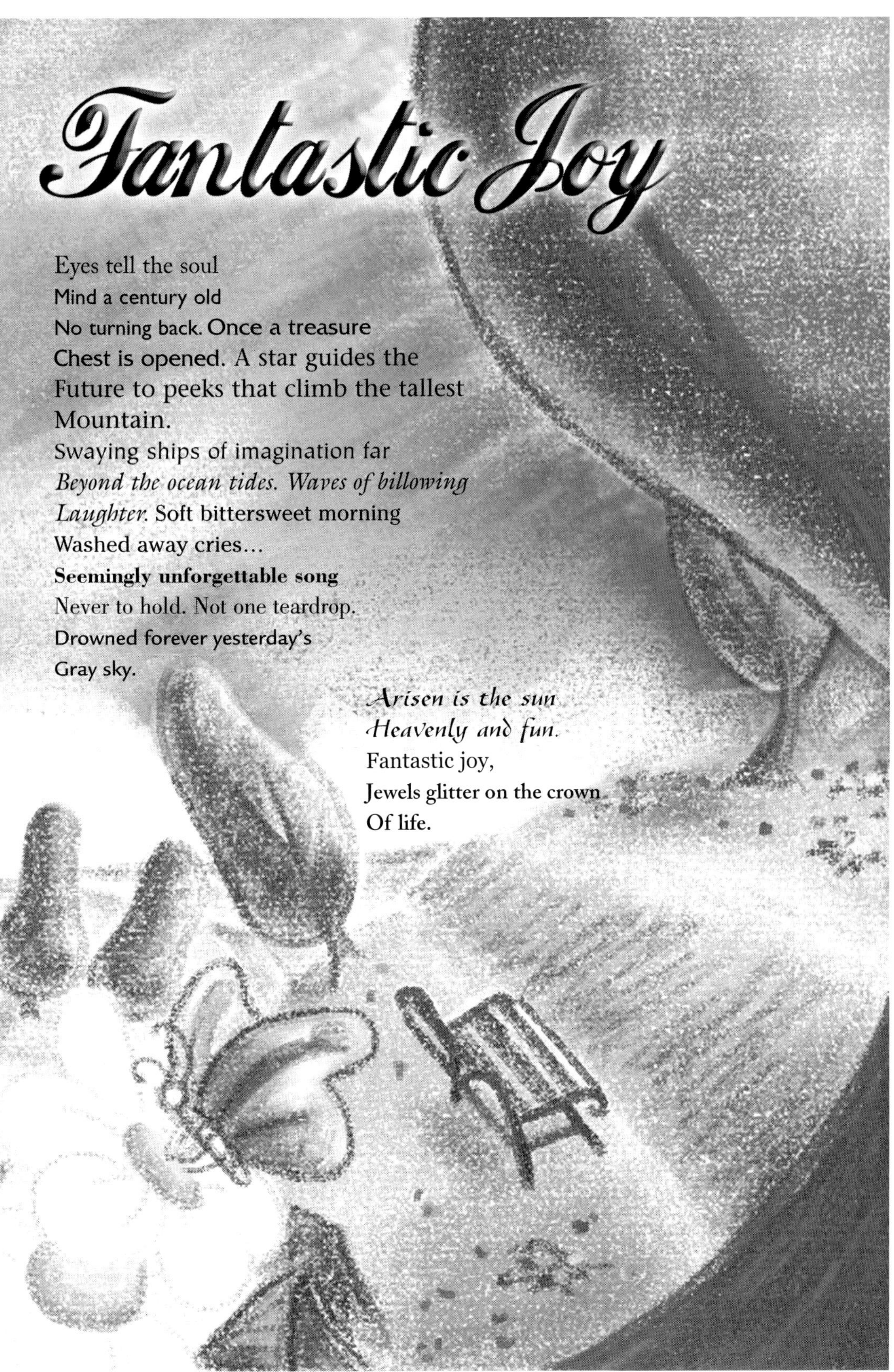

Fantastic Joy

Eyes tell the soul
Mind a century old
No turning back. Once a treasure
Chest is opened. A star guides the
Future to peeks that climb the tallest
Mountain.
Swaying ships of imagination far
Beyond the ocean tides. Waves of billowing
Laughter. Soft bittersweet morning
Washed away cries…
Seemingly unforgettable song
Never to hold. Not one teardrop.
Drowned forever yesterday's
Gray sky.

Arisen is the sun
Heavenly and fun.
Fantastic joy,
Jewels glitter on the crown
Of life.

I Have Run

I have run through the tides
Of sorrow and danced with the wolves
Swept away by peace. The musical
Stories began to unfold and
Remnants of this dreary darkened
Room began to fade away.
Life beholds the grandest dreams
For all to share . . .
Cherry Blossoms guide the ship
Blackbirds and Robins
In the dazzling land of . . .
Blossoms of joy
No holding back just like the cool
Breeze—All that is meant to be
A shining star dancing on
My pillow
On a moonlit night
Is all that
Our hearts
Must share.

Saturday Afternoon

Saturday afternoon…_The sun
Isn't shining and I'm alone_
Except you're in my dreams.
My daydreams, which are raining
Down on this darkened room!

What's up chocolate martini?
If this is part of the wine
of life…
Well, sir…I'll just skip
This favor.

No more dreary rooms and sitting
Alone…Although, the relaxing
Part is all right and having
You near is wonderful.

But…Can you think of more
To be enjoyed?

Once we're out there
Climbing the trees **and**
Eating the apples of
Life.

Over and Over Again

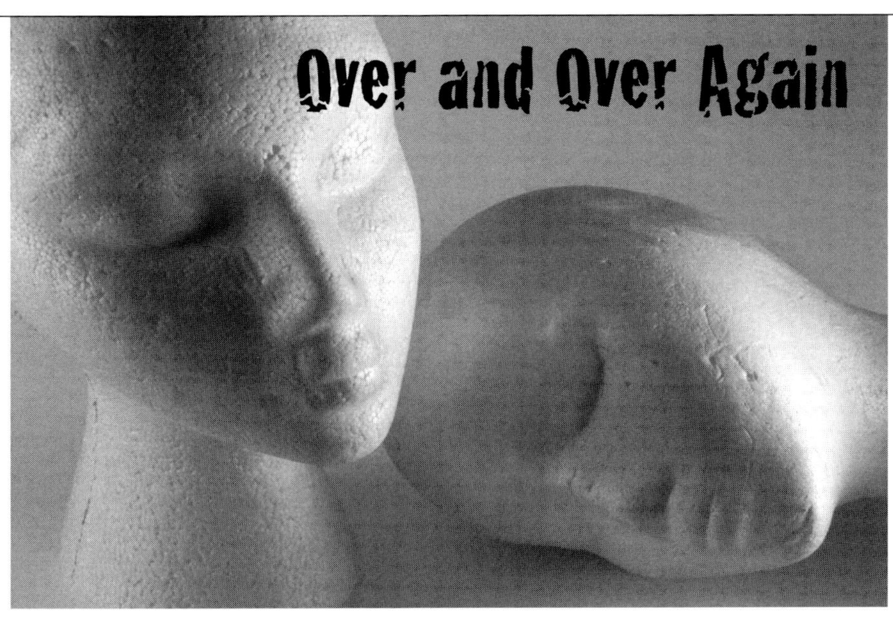

Yesterday seemingly unforgettable song. The
Darkness won't seem to melt these teardrops
Forever into the ocean waves. No holding
Back. Just have to have you near is all I need
No letting go. Troubled by silent whispers
Is forever in my heart.
No turning back. No erasing the pain. No hands to
Hold. Just lonesome, I feel so alone...love...
Simple feelings that take us and once it
Embeds our soul there is no turning
Back. No one can erase memories and
Beautiful times shared.
No one...*Pain comes with love and
Morning is near. And as the waves part.*
The ocean fills us with strength
To move on. Shameless beautiful to
Touch without feeling, have to start
Over. All I've created, All I've destroyed...
And over and over again.
What I've learned I've started over again
Back when before.
The ocean's brought us together again
Never part just come closed to my heart.

So that tomorrow can begin
Over and over again.

EVERYTHING IS ONE

Everything is one.
No matter where I go or how
Far I climb all the dreams
Shatter in my eyes. Heaven knows
I've seen ancient cries and
The moon burning bright.
The night appears and the morning
Is soon to come.
Chains have been woven endlessly about.
The ending is near.
Peace guides the journey. Arisen is the sun
Life dances on the ocean waves

Chance seemingly never fades away
Obstacles are overcome.
Joy seized and kissed the hands
Of time.
Music is that forest that
Never stops. Rhythm shocks my Mind.
Psychedelic or sky
Painted blue
Doesn't matter.

Just as long as all my
Dreams come true.

The End

Love

Jimmy

Robinson's astoundingly positive attitude and musical stories were of paramount importance when he found himself cast into a predicament so horrible, it would coerce most people to relinquish all hope. Call it the world of forgotten souls, but Jimmy could never forget such a natural proclivity toward the creative endeavors. It was through these imaginative channels that he was able to propel himself from an average obscure number to inventor of the musical stories.

The Author